THE ACA LEGAL SERIES

Volume 11

"LEGAL ISSUES
IN LICENSURE"

THE ACA LEGAL SERIES:

Series Editor: Theodore P. Remley, Jr., JD, PhD

THE ACA LEGAL SERIES

Volume 11

"LEGAL ISSUES IN LICENSURE"

Donald Anderson, EdD
Carl D. Swanson, JD, EdD

Series Editor
Theodore P. Remley, Jr., JD, PhD

10 9 8 7 6 5 4 3 2 1

American Counseling Association
5999 Stevenson Avenue
Alexandria, VA 22304

Director of Communications
Jennifer L. Sacks

Acquisitions and Development Editor
Carolyn Baker

Production/Design Manager
Michael Comlish

Copyeditor
Lucy Blanton

Library of Congress Cataloging-in-Publication Data

Anderson, Donald, 1946–
    Legal issues in licensure / Donald Anderson, Carl D. Swanson.
        p. cm. — (ACA legal series ; v. 11)
    Includes bibliographical references.
    ISBN 1-55620-129-X
    1. Counselors—Licenses—United States. 2. Counseling—Law and legislation—United States. I. Swanson, Carl D. II. Title. III. Series
KF2910.P751A53   1994
344.73'01761361323—dc20   93-33196
[347.3041761361323]   CIP

Contents

Contents

Biographies

Donald Anderson is a professor in the Counselor Education Department at Radford University, Radford, Virginia. He has over 13 years of experience in private practice as a licensed professional counselor in Roanoke. He has served on both the Virginia Board of Professional Counselors and the Board of Health Professions for over 8 years. From 1990 to 1992, he served as chair of the Board of Professional Counselors, and he currently chairs the board's Scope and Standards of Practice Committee. He was a member of the ACA Task Force on Impaired Practitioners. Dr. Anderson is a Certified Clinical Mental Health Counselor and a National Certified Career Counselor. He received his EdD from Virginia Polytechnic Institute and State University in 1977. In 1993, he received the Chi Sigma Iota Outstanding Practitioner Award at the ACA convention in Atlanta, Georgia.

Carl D. Swanson is a professor emeritus at James Madison University in Harrisonburg, Virginia, where he coordinated the Counselor Education Program. Dr. Swanson has a private practice specializing in addiction counseling in Grottoes, Virginia. He was the first chair of the Counselor Certification Committee established by the Virginia Legislature in 1975 and of the Virginia Counselor Licensure Board established in 1976, serving a total of 10 years on both credentialing bodies. He also chaired the National Board for Certified Counselors and the

licensure commission of the Virginia Counselors Association
and the American Counseling Association. Dr. Swanson is a
licensed professional counselor and has practiced law in Missouri and Virginia. He received his JD from Washington and Lee
University and his EdD from Western Michigan University.

· **Theodore P. Remley, Jr.,** Series Editor, is Executive Director of the American Counseling Association. Immediately prior
to assuming this position, Dr. Remley was chair of the Department of Counselor Education at Mississippi State University in
Starkville. He holds a PhD from the Department of Counselor
Education at the University of Florida in Gainesville and a JD
in law from the Catholic University of America in Washington,
DC.

Preface

Counselor credentialing can be confusing to counseling students as well as counseling practitioners. Counselor credentialing continues in a state of flux, even though basic requirements have stayed fairly constant. There is as yet no definitive set of national standards applicable within and among states. Some states certify or register counselors in addition to licensure. State examinations are not yet uniform; state application forms vary widely; and there is neither full nor partial reciprocity among states. Voluntary professional associations, such as the National Board for Certified Counselors (NBCC), also issue credentials in the form of certification. However, each counselor credentialing entity has differing requirements, responsibilities, and privileges.

Counselors must be able to answer intelligently the question, "What credentials do I need?" Practicing professionals and counseling students need to be aware of their state's requirements as well as the national educational core requirements recommended for counselors. Keeping up to date is essential in order to better meet future professional challenges. Fully understanding the differing state statutes that legally influence a counseling practice is imperative.

This monograph in the ACA Legal Series aims to clarify the meaning, value, and drawbacks of each type of credential. Counselors need to decide which credentials are desirable or are legally necessary and which will enhance their professional credibility, standing, and development. Our analysis of the various credentials should help counselors to make informed choices.

This monograph may also be useful in counselor training program professional identity courses. The credential analyses presented here can help students in deciding upon their career direction and upon the level of training and amount of supervised experience needed to attain their professional goals.

Above all, the authors hope that this monograph will stimulate thinking about credentialing—and the credentialing maze.

Glossary

Certification: The second highest level of state regulation. The term *certification* tells the public that an individual has met professional requirements and may practice in a specific area. National voluntary credentialing agencies also use the term *certification* to signify that the professional has met certain standards promulgated by the profession.

Credential: A certificate, granted by a recognized authority or credible professional agency, showing evidence of the holder's education, training, or experience in a specific profession or field.

Inspection: The lowest level and least restrictive form of state regulation. This is a procedure whereby on-site inspections of professional practice are made by appropriate state agencies.

Licensure: The highest form of credentialing adopted by a state. Licensure normally protects a professional title, such as professional counselor, and defines the scope of practice allowable. Requirements are usually higher than those for certification or registration, and more privileges accompany this credential. In those states that require licensure for counseling, a professional must be licensed in order to engage in the practice of counseling.

National Voluntary Credential: Generally takes the form of certification showing a level of education, training, or experience achieved by the certificant. These credentials are granted by a national professional association or certifying agency and are not a legal requirement for practice.

Reciprocity: The full acceptance by one state of another state's licensure or certification, which permits a person with a valid license in one state to move to another state and, upon application, receive licensure in that state. Even where there is no reciprocity, states may accept the results of written exams used by other states or national certifying agencies. States also may accept a credential from another state as evidence that certain requirements for licensure, certification, or registration have been met.

Registration: The second lowest level of state regulation. In this procedure, a member of a profession simply registers as one practicing a specific profession. When states specify educational or training requirements that a person must meet in order to be registered, what is termed *registration* is actually certification.

State Credential: A legal document issued by state governments that governs the practice of a profession within the boundaries of the issuing state. Credentials regulate a profession for the purpose of protecting the public.

Sunset Legislation: A state statute requiring professional boards to justify their continued existence or cease functioning.

What Is a Professional Credential?

Over the past two decades, legislators and counselors, recognizing that counseling needed to be brought under control of law, have sought and achieved regulation of the profession. They accomplished this objective by creating credentialing. Bills were introduced into and passed by legislatures, and signed into law by state governors. Credentials enacted include licensure, certification, registration, and inspection. Professional counselor organizations also began issuing credentials signifying specific professional status.

Counselors clearly need to be aware of the benefits and disadvantages of professional regulations through credentialing. Yet according to a recent study (Alberding, Lauver, & Patnoe, 1993, p. 33), most counselors are "unfamiliar with potential negative consequences of regulation" although most are "desirous of more information regarding these issues."

To promote counselor awareness, this chapter focuses on the following questions: What does credentialing do? What are its benefits? What are the criticisms of the credentialing process? Who gains and who loses because of credentialing? How can practicing counselors and counseling students decide for which credential to apply? In answering these questions, this chapter first looks at what credentialing does, what benefits it brings. Criticisms of the credentialing process, including cost, restrictiveness, and complexity, are then explored and answered. Finally, questions for practicing counselors and counseling students to ask themselves in deciding what credentials to apply for are provided.

The Benefits of Credentialing

Credentialing is an essential mechanism for communicating to the public assurances of minimal standards of education, training, and experience. The public is also assured by the governmental or nongovernmental body granting the credential that an attempt is made to ensure that unethical, negligent, or incompetent practitioners will be restricted or denied the privilege of professional practice. In other words, credentials give persons seeking the services of a professional counselor a degree of confidence in the credentialed counselor they choose.

Credentialing helps to educate the public about mental health services. Ethical standards legally require practitioners to adhere to truth in advertising, limiting their claims of expertise only to those areas of practice in which they have training, experience, or relevant educational degrees. Professional credentials often specify areas of practice in which the holder is qualified to practice. As Romano (1992) suggested, credentialing provides information to the consumer and also provides an identity for the counselor. Credentialing as a means of providing information to the public and clarifying professional identity clearly has benefits for the general public, the profession, and the individual practitioner. From the public's perspective, credentialing certainly seems to assist consumers of counseling services in making informed choices from among the ever-increasing array of mental health service providers.

Credentials help the public identify legitimate counselors. Professionals who have met state requirements or national professional association criteria for a credential have, minimally, a core knowledge base and have taken the initiative to obtain a credential. This is often a time-consuming and expensive procedure that shows the individual's dedication to professionalism.

Ultimately, how a professional counselor functions and is perceived by the general public is a result of six interrelated factors that include (1) how the profession and the role of the counselor are defined; (2) the specialty designation of the practicing counselor, such as community mental health counselor, school counselor, rehabilitation counselor, substance abuse counselor, or marriage and family counselor; (3) consumer expectations associated with a particular role and function; (4) regulatory controls such as state licensure or voluntary national professional certification; (5) statutory definitions; and (6) professional ethics and prevailing standards of practice.

The profession itself is generally enhanced through the gradual upgrading of professional standards that takes place over time. Increasing awareness of practice standards as well as increasing professional competition for jobs, income, and prestige all contribute to increased, rather than decreased, qualifications for credentials in counseling and other mental health professions. Ethical standards of all credentialed professions make statements that professionals may offer only those services for which they are qualified by training or experience.

Among compelling reasons for obtaining a state credential are the opening of career options such as private practice, which may require a license (Remley, 1991), and the fact that in many states privileged communication is only legally guaranteed to clients who are treated by a credentialed professional. Credentials announce to governmental bodies, administrators, colleagues, and the public that professional counselors are legitimate, qualified professionals. It is important to note that exemptions allowing a counselor to practice today without a license could be gone tomorrow by a simple act of the legislature.

If national credentials are voluntary, why should the professional counselor bother with them? Why become a National Certified Counselor (NCC), Certified Clinical Mental Health Counselor (CCMHC), or Certified Rehabilitation Counselor (CRC)? An ACA *Guidepost* article (Remley, 1992) answered this question by stating that voluntary national credentials have been created so professional counselors can verify they have obtained the minimum knowledge and experience needed for the competent practice of counseling. Without voluntary national credentialing, those who have no understanding of our field, including state legislators or employers, would be the ones deciding the minimum standards for professional counselor education and experience.

Legitimate credentials indicate that counselors who hold them have much more than a minimal education. The more counselors who hold and use their credentials in their practice, the more educated the public will become about professional counseling credentials. Eventually, well-educated consumers will demand that professional counselors hold legitimate professional counselor credentials. Although a state license or certificate may be necessary for a practice or job, these mandatory credentials do not demonstrate support for minimum national standards that have been developed by counselors. Achievement of a legitimate credential provides demonstrable support for national standards in the counseling profession.

Criticisms of Credentialing

The cost of credentials has been the source of constant criticism. Annually, counselors generally pay relatively little for the rights and privileges that are conferred by a license or certificate. First, the fee goes only to cover actual administrative and enforcement costs. It is expensive to investigate complaints of unethical or negligent behavior. However, this investigative function protects not only the public but also the legitimate professional counselor. Enforcement, investigative, and hearing dollars are well spent. Initial fees, including examination fees, are also relatively inexpensive when their use and purpose are weighed.

That credentialing is too restrictive was one of the earliest arguments used in opposition to credentialing. When it becomes necessary to hold a particular credential in order to practice a profession, individuals who might be qualified in the field through a nontraditional process are not allowed to practice. This negative aspect of credentialing must be acknowledged and is the price paid for protecting society.

There has been a tendency for credentialing boards in the past to raise their standards continually, resulting in charges of elitism. This movement toward raising entry-level requirements is something the profession itself must monitor. Those already licensed often think in terms of dollars when drafting revisions of qualifications: If fewer professionals are allowed to practice, there is less marketplace competition. Striking a happy medium between minimal professional standards to insure the highest quality of services possible and overly restrictive standards that could exclude qualified professionals and raise costs will always be a challenge to mental health professionals.

Complexity has been another objection to credentialing. Actually, the application requirements for credentials are relatively simple and fairly uniform throughout the counseling profession. Representative of what usually is required are the following:

- an application with an application fee
- letters of reference
- transcripts showing 45 to 60 graduate credit hours in counseling or a closely related field including a graduate degree
- evidence of specific course work, which is spelled out by each state board and generally includes counseling theories, counseling techniques, group dynamics, career development, assessment and measurement, research, abnormal psychology, and human growth and development
- documented supervision of practice of usually 2,000 to 4,000 clock hours with 1 hour of face-to-face supervision for each 20 hours spent with clients
- a written examination that is taken after all other requirements have been met. The boards notify the applicants of the time and place of the examination.

Maintenance requirements generally consist of documentation of a specified number of continuing education units or credits earned each year plus a renewal fee. There seems to be a trend toward yearly professional updating, a standard set by the National Board for Certified Counselors in its first year of operation.

Questions for Deciding to Apply for a Credential

Practicing counselors and counseling students are advised to study each credential available in the field and then answer the following questions:

- **Is this credential mandatory?** Must I have this particular credential in order to practice my profession? Do I need the credential in order to practice? Will this credential help my client get reimbursed for my services or will it help me get promoted within my agency? In some cases and states the answer might be "no" to these questions. However, in some states a license is required to practice counseling, and statutes require insurance companies to reimburse clients who receive counseling services from licensed professional counselors.

- **Will a voluntary credential, such as the one offered by the National Board for Certified Counselors or the Commission on Rehabilitation Counselor Certification (CRCC), be helpful to me professionally?** In most cases the answer is "yes." Even in states with licensure, other professional certification shows the public, and more specifically potential clients, that you have taken additional steps to become nationally recognized in your profession. It lets fellow professionals know of your concern for and dedication to your profession. Such a credential can also be helpful in your professional advertising or helpful within your institution, demonstrating evidence of your professional advancement or achievement. The counseling profession created NBCC and CRCC and established the standards for the profession and therefore should be supported. The profession cannot allow state legislators, who are not professional counselors, to define our profession.

- **Do changes need to be made in credentials that are presently available?** Ask yourself, "Are the credentials available really a help to me or relevant to what I do professionally?" There is probably a generic credential that is professionally beneficial or appropriate. However, in some cases, no existing credential relates directly to your counseling specialty, area of interest, or expertise. If this is your case, suggest to appropriate credentialing bodies that a specialty credential be developed. Work for this or any other changes you may determine are needed. Suggest changes in existing credentialing requirements or regulations as well. Express your perceived need.

Educational Credentials

There are three basic categories of credentialing: educational credentialing, national voluntary credentialing, and state regulatory credentialing. This chapter looks at educational credentials. The next two chapters explore national and state credentials.

Credentialing in the counseling profession begins with professional training in colleges and universities. Through professional education, counselors begin the process of preparing to meet qualification and performance standards of the profession. Programs that accredit professional training programs are a key component in the process of assuring quality in the profession of counseling. The dimensions of educational program accreditation related to the counseling profession are diverse.

Graduation from an accredited college or university is the basic requirement for entry into a professional field. State credentialing bodies and national associations engaged in issuing credentials do not want to risk giving a stamp of approval to a person whose degree may have come from a mail order catalog, where there may be no check on the quality of the education.

Accrediting agencies for higher education are usually regional in nature. These regions, such as Southern, North Central, or Western, are composed of those schools and colleges in their geographic area that are concerned about the quality of education. Inspection teams sent to the member institutions periodically evaluate the practices of the institution. If established standards are met by the college or university, it can advertise that it is accredited by the regional association. Regional accreditation is considered essential for a college or university to be considered a legitimate institution of higher education.

Specialized accrediting agencies for graduate programs are national in nature and recognized widely within the professional area in which they operate. The graduate program accrediting agencies for counselor training programs are the Council on Rehabilitation Education, Inc. (CORE) and the Council for Accreditation of Counseling and Related Programs (CACREP). They are the specialized accrediting agencies recognized by the counseling profession.

CACREP grew from early standards set by the Association for Counselor Education and Supervision (ACES), a division of ACA, to improve and facilitate uniformity in counselor education programs. Each accredited program requires 48 semester hours covering eight core areas of skill, knowledge, and clinical application. These areas are virtually identical with NBCC and state credentialing board requirements (and are listed here for prospective applicants to use in evaluating requirements of their graduate training programs):

1. **human growth and development** (the nature and needs of individuals at all developmental levels)
2. **social and cultural foundations** (issues and trends in a multicultural and diverse society)
3. **helping relationships** (counseling and consultation processes)
4. **groups** (group development, dynamics of group counseling theories, and group counseling methods and skills)
5. **career and life-style development** (career development and the interrelationships among work, family, and other life factors)
6. **appraisal** (individual and group approaches to assessment and evaluation)
7. **research and program evaluation** (types of research methods, basic statistics, and ethical and legal considerations in research)

8. **professional orientation** (all aspects of professional functioning including history, roles, organizational structures, ethics, standards, and credentialing).

Other core requirements include supervised practicums and internships. Also included are doctoral-level standards as well as additional specialized curricular experiences for programs in clinical counseling, community mental health counseling, marriage and family counseling/therapy, school counseling, student development counseling, administration in higher education, and student development counseling in higher education.

CORE is the accrediting body granting recognition to master's degree programs in rehabilitation counselor education. CORE's standards for program approval are similar to those of CACREP. Although rehabilitation counseling focuses on the rehabilitation of physical disability, CORE's accreditation body also assures quality standards in areas of counseling for emotional, mental, and behavioral disorders.

 # National Voluntary Credentials

The second type of credential is national and voluntary. These credentials, supported by professional associations such as the American Counseling Association, provide their members professional identity and credibility. The national voluntary credentials for counseling professionals are based on codes of ethics, standards of practice, and qualifications for membership or affiliation established by ACA and its divisions, and they "give the general public a set of standards to measure the profession and its practitioners" (Clawson, 1991, p. 1). Although a professional association like ACA is not a governmental agency, and membership is voluntary (and highly encouraged) but not required by law, such national voluntary credentials represent the confirmation of a professional counselor's training and experience.

The national voluntary credentials also reflect the prestige and standing of ACA and the private agencies it has created and supports for both generic and specialty credentials. These credentialing agencies include the National Board for Certified Counselors, "chartered as an avenue of public trust and protection" (Clawson, 1991, p. 1). The NBCC issues the National Certified Counselor (NCC) credential, which is considered generic certification and which is based on its entry-level requirements. The NBCC also grants specialty certification, including the National Certified Career Counselor (NCCC), National Certified School Counselor (NCSC), National Certified Gerontological Counselor (NCGC), and Certified Clinical Mental Health Counselor (CCMHC). In order to ensure that reviews of qualifications of applicants for certification are conducted in an impartial and fair manner, NBCC today operates as a free-standing, totally independent board.

The impact of NBCC has been tremendous. Nearly 18,000 counselors have been certified since its inception. In addition, as of May 1993, 32 of the 39 state boards used the NBCC-developed National Counselor Examination (NCE) in their states for licensure.

Another agency offering national voluntary credentials to counselors and important in defining standards and functions of professional counselors for the public has been the National Academy of Certified Clinical Mental Health Counselors (NACCMHC). The academy, established by the American Mental Health Counselors Association, was in the forefront in setting a national standard for the clinical mental health counselor in private practice. Certification requirements for the Certified Clinical Mental Health Counselor credential were increased beyond the traditional entry-level standard to 60 graduate credit hours in 1992. As of July 1, 1993, the academy merged with the NBCC, and the CCMHC credential is now a specialty granted by the board (NBCC, 1993).

In addition to the national voluntary generic and specialty credentials issued by the NBCC are other private counseling specialty certifications developed outside the standards and influence of the American Counseling Association. These include those offered by the Commission on Rehabilitation Counselor Certification, the National Association of Alcoholism and Drug Abuse Counselors (NAADAC), the National Association of Social Workers (NASW), and the American Association for Marriage and Family Therapy (AAMFT).

The Commission on Rehabilitation Counselor Certification issues for those practicing in the rehabilitation field the Certified Rehabilitation Counselor (CRC) credential. This specialty certificate was established before NBCC was created and has been widely received in the field. Since 1974, many job openings offered by public and private rehabilitation organizations have required this CRC credential.

The National Association of Alcoholism and Drug Abuse Counselors entered the field of certification in 1990 as it announced the "establishment of a new national credential to be identified as the National Certified Addiction Counselor (NCAC)." The association noted that its

> purpose in creating the NCAC is to provide a credential for competent alcoholism and drug abuse counselors that will bring them the national recognition they deserve. . . .NAADAC will advocate for the credential at the national level with legislators, third-party payers, and other health care professionals. (NAADAC, 1990)

The first exam for this NCAC credential in 1991 was offered at 60 sites in 45 states, and over 8,000 professionals became certified NCACs (NAADAC), 1991). This certification at the national voluntary level is unique in that the applicant must first hold state certification. NAADAC stresses that this is a competency-based advanced-level credential. In the past, national professional certification has generally preceded the availability of state credentials. Further, the requirements are more demanding for this national credential than for the state credentials. It should be noted that a graduate degree is not a requirement in this field for counselor certification.

The National Association of Social Workers created the Academy of Certified Social Workers (ASCW) in 1960. Applicants have to be NASW members, have 2 years of postmaster's experience, and, since 1972, pass a national exam. The American Board of Examiners on Clinical Social Work (ABECSW) was later established "to develop certification of highly skilled social work practitioners by a board of their peers" (Garcia, 1990). The status of diplomate is now awarded to these professionals. With state regulation, the future of this prestigious credential is in doubt.

The American Association for Marriage and Family Therapy offers clinical membership for its highly trained members. Efforts of this association are now being directed toward securing state credentialing for its members.

Many other counseling specialty credentials have been established. Professional counselors must carefully evaluate each specialty credential to determine whether it is legitimate and whether it will be accepted by the profession and the public as an indicator of specialty expertise.

 # State Regulatory Credentials

The third type of credential is state and regulatory. All states, U.S. possessions, and the District of Columbia have a variety of professions—such as harbor pilots, accountants, nurses, physical therapists, security guards, physicians, morticians, veterinarians, school social workers, real estate brokers, school counselors—for which a credential is offered.

Within state governments, several administrative departments are charged with the issuance of credentials. Typically the state department of education certifies school personnel, including teachers, school psychologists, school counselors, and administrators. Departments of health or professional and occupational regulation credential other professions.

Forms of State Regulation

The forms of regulation or credentialing in states, ranging from least to most restrictive, are inspection, registration, certification, and licensure.

Inspection. The lowest, least restrictive level of regulation is inspection, in which a state agency periodically examines the activities and premises of practitioners of an occupation or profession to determine if the practitioner is conducting the occupation or profession in a manner consistent with public safety, health, and welfare.

The state also periodically inspects the practice of professionals who hold state credentials. The states have reserved this right to better protect the public. State inspectors do not have to wait for a complaint to be filed but may visit a counselor's office at any time to determine if his or her practice is within professional boundaries and adhering to the ethical standards of the profession.

Registration. The next level of regulation is registration, in which the practitioner of an occupation or profession may be required to submit evidence of minimum education or training in the chosen field and submit information concerning the location, nature, and operation of practice. For example, in some states registered professionals must provide proof of a bachelor's level degree in their field and the name and address of their current employer.

Professional entry standards are not generally established for registration processes. Typically, registrants provide limited demographic and background information and the location of occupational activity. Education and training requirements vary. Those that exist serve to establish minimal differentiation of the registered professional from counseling work in general. Several states currently describe their credentialed counselors as *registered*. For example, counselors are titled registered professional counselors in Kansas and registered practicing counselors in North Carolina. In both cases, because the titles are protected, counselors are technically certified counselors based on the definition of statutory certification.

Certification. The second highest level of state regulation is certification. At this level the states begin to move into the skills area. Many—but not all—state certifying boards require an examination. Typically a certificate states that the person to whom it is issued has the minimum skills and training needed to engage properly in a certain profession (or occupation) and, generally, that there are no known character defects or other impediments that will interfere with practice of the profession.

For one professional counseling specialty—school counseling—certification is required in all states with relatively uniform educational and experiential standards. Most require a master's degree in counseling, course work in professional identity, and a practicum at the school level at which the person wants to practice, e.g., at the elementary level for future practice in the elementary school. Some state departments of education also require a teaching certificate as a prerequisite for counselor certification, although historically counselors have not supported such a requirement.

Certification also provides title protection. That is, only those persons who are, for example, Certified Rehabilitation Counselors may hold themselves out to the public as rehabilitation counselors or as persons practicing rehabilitation counseling. With great variation among the states, certification also generally protects the titles of professional counselor and mental health counselor. The term *counselor* standing alone has not yet been protected because of the many types of counseling available—from weight loss counseling to used car counseling.

Licensure. The highest level of state regulation is licensure. Requirements for a license are generally more stringent than for other state credentials. Examinations (sometimes as many as three) are required by boards of professional counselors. These may consist of short answer, essay, and oral exams as well as the examination of transcripts and references. The educational and experiential requirements for licensure have traditionally been higher than for certification or registration. An exception is Maryland, where the counselor certification law has higher requirements than several state licensure laws.

Licensure, like certification, provides title protection. Licensure also protects the practice of counseling within the state; and licensure laws define and protect the scope of counseling practice as well as the title of the practitioner.

Why States Regulate Counseling

State regulation of the counseling profession through licensure, certification, or registration achieves some basic societal and professional goals. These include (1) protecting the public from potential harm, (2) enhancing consumer freedom of choice in selecting service providers, and (3) excluding practitioners who do not meet reasonable standards of professional preparation and practice. However, a balance needs to be maintained among public protection, consumer freedom of choice, and reasonable standards of professional preparation and practice. A functional partnership between state regulatory agencies, professional associations, and other groups is the key to meeting the ideal of a well-regulated profession that both protects and serves the public welfare.

The complexities and conflicts that exist concerning public access to mental health services raise such questions as (1) Are standards being set at such a high level as to restrict access to professionals? (2) Does regulation actually protect the public from harm inherent in counseling and therapy? Within these questions is the complex legal and professional issue of occupational regulation and freedom of choice.

In many states the ideals of negotiated and reconciled roles and responsibilities and of cooperative efforts to serve and protect the public interest has been achieved. Virginia is an example of cooperation among the legislature, the Department of Health Professions Boards, the Board of Professional Counselors, ACA state and ACA state-division associations, and other groups working cooperatively and effectively to balance the needs for public protection and for professional standards and ideals (Anderson, 1993).

Licensure, Certification, and Registration Statutes

State regulations that may restrict market access to providers and consumers of counseling services can take several forms. Governmental agencies use licensure, certification, and registration as regulatory mechanisms for varying levels of control over a profession. Which is most useful or meaningful? Can consumers benefit from knowing the distinctions among a licensed counselor, a certified counselor, and a registered counselor? What does a plaque or certificate from a government agency, professional association, or other issuing group mean? What does a consumer see on the office wall of a professional counselor?

Confusion exists in the counseling profession and in the minds of the public because of inconsistent use by governmental and nongovernmental bodies of licensure, certification and registration terminology. For example, in Rhode Island and Maryland counselors are certified, but in Oklahoma and Oregon they are licensed. Counselors in Oregon and Maryland perform essentially the same function as counselors in Virginia and Louisiana, but in Virginia and Louisiana the title and scope of practice are defined and protected by the license. To add to the confusion, any group selling a product or service may establish a certification process for that product or service—as has been the case with testing services and such various modalities of counseling as hypnosis, biofeedback, and transcendental meditation.

Summarizing the common meanings of terms used in regulating the counseling profession may be helpful. A state occupational **license** affords protection of a professional title and scope of practice. Licensure laws are called *occupational or professional practice acts* because these statutes define a process (meeting qualifications) through which individuals are granted the privilege of or permission to engage in specific occupational activity and to refer to themselves by a specific occupational title. The effect of counselor licensure is the establishment of state control over a professional title and scope of professional activity.

A profession can also control the use of a specific title by a process of **certification**. Governmental agencies grant certification to counselors who meet established criteria to engage in counseling practice. Statutory certification, a certification process that carries the weight of governmental authority, is exemplified by an Arizona law (1988, amended 1989), which protects the title of certified counselor, and a Maryland statute (1985), which protects the title certified professional counselor. The statutes under which a counselor seeks the privilege to use those titles also define qualifications necessary for authority to use the titles. No noncertified individual can use those titles within the jurisdictions of Arizona and Maryland. However, although the scope of counseling practices is defined in Arizona, Maryland, and other states that certify counselors, the scope of practice is generally not protected by statutory definition. Statutory certification is a privilege that authenticates counselor qualifications. It also may restrict the use of a professional title.

Registration is a third form of regulation. It permits members of a profession to be registered with the state if they possess

minimum credentials, thereby enabling them to practice their
profession.

State Licensure Protections and Privileges

In the profession of counseling, the achievement of true practice
protection is almost impossible due to the overlap among the
behavioral science professions of clinical social work, counseling
psychology, clinical psychology, and professional counseling.

Although the function of counseling and psychotherapy may
be a core component of the scope of practice of counseling,
psychology, or clinical social work, the training traditions,
clinical requirements, and areas of treatment focus vary. Each
of the behavioral sciences draws from the same body of research,
philosophy, and theory. Each group conducts its practice using
a common therapeutic milieu. Historical professional roots,
training traditions, and philosophical orientation to assessment and treatment vary among the groups and are reflected in
differences in the licensing process and requirements. However,
there is considerable overlap in scope of practice. True discrimination among scopes of practice within psychology, clinical
social work, and counseling is illusive and essentially impossible. The consequence of insisting on differences that in actu-
ality do not exist causes needless confusion for the consuming
public and leads to legislative turf battles as professional
groups attempt to carve out an area of practice that excludes
other behavioral science professionals. However, although true
practice protection is impossible within the behavioral sciences,
the claim for practice protection among the behavioral science
professionals seems justifiable. Therefore, licensing laws within
the behavioral science profession truly represent title protection associated with a common and shared scope of practice by
counseling, psychology, and social work.

Privileges that may come to the professional counselor with
licensure can be illustrated by those attained in the state of
Virginia. The first was title protection. Only licensees could hold
themselves out as licensed professional counselors. Five subse-
quent privileges came slowly and required intensive, expensive
lobbying efforts that included educating the state government

(courts, legislature, and administrative departments) on the role, function, and capabilities of the professional counselor.

One of the later achieved privileges was inclusion as a licensed health provider, which opened many doors. Two more were that licensed counselors were permitted to provide testing services for the schools and other agencies (by action of the Virginia Attorney General) and to use the terms *therapy* and *psychotherapy*. These terms, which had been traditionally reserved to the psychiatrist or psychologist, are now used by all behavioral science professionals, including licensed professional counselors.

Another privilege was that licensed counselors were included in the privileged communication statute along with psychiatrists, psychologists, and clinical social workers. A final privilege was that licensed counselors were included in freedom-of-choice legislation, which prohibits insurers from discrimination against them in reimbursing for mental health treatment (Code of Virginia, 1987).

Today, licensed professional counselors have attained these privileges in other states as well as Virginia. Changes taking place now in the area of mental health treatment brought about by rising costs and the advent of health maintenance organizations (HMOs) and self-insured corporations are drastically changing this, as is seen in the chapter discussing third-party reimbursements and cost consciousness.

Licensure Boards

The purpose of a counselor licensing board is to promulgate rules, policies, and procedures in the form of professional regulations to ensure that public health, safety, and welfare are protected. This is accomplished through a process by which a board, acting by authority of law, grants a privilege to an individual to engage in professional activity or practice that has statutory definition as a practice act and that carries a protected professional title.

Boards that credential counselors represent an interface between the counseling profession and the consuming public. On the one hand, the board's primary concern is the protection of the public from a high risk of harm attributable to the nature of mental health counseling and the vulnerability of clients in the counseling process. On the other hand, the board is confronted with understanding the scope of counseling practice, the standards of professional preparation, and the ethical codes and practice standards of various professional groups with which its licensees are associated. A board must reconcile and balance the need to serve the public's interest and protect public health, safety, and welfare with (1) the ideals of the profession as expressed in its ethical code, scope of clinical practice, and qualifications and in its requirements for entry into the profession; and (2) a board's legal mandate to establish the minimal standards necessary for entry to a regulated profession so as not to violate a person's right to choose to engage in the profession of counseling (or other profession, trade, or occupation) as protected by the U. S. and state constitutions.

The rights of individual counseling professionals, the ideals and standards of the profession, and the statutory authority to protect public interest represent the multiple focuses of the regulatory activity of boards of professional counselors. Balancing these interests and concerns while establishing regulatory policy and procedures that are lawful is a difficult task. Because most board members are unpaid volunteers, the challenge is to find qualified, concerned, and dedicated persons to assume membership on regulatory boards.

Creating, Changing, and Maintaining Regulations

In addition to administering and reviewing credentials, certifying examinations, conducting disciplinary investigations, and adjudicating complaints, one of the most important functions of a regulatory board is overseeing the legal process of regulatory review, revision, and promulgation. This process is considered central to professional regulation. Regulatory issues and concerns that become the focus of regulatory review and modifications include the following:

- The profession of counseling is in a constant state of evolution. Standards of practice are changing to reflect, for example, the emergence of dual relationships as a central issue in professional ethics and the increasing incidence of professional impairment related to sexual improprieties and substance abuse. Other areas of significant change in professional standards are treatment planning and standards of care issues.
- Ethical standards are changing and need to be translated into enforceable regulatory standards that both reflect the ideals of the profession and conform to statutory definitions of the profession. Legal precedents that provide a basis for refinement of standards of ethics and standards of counseling

practice must be translated into regulatory policy. Professional disclosure and informed consent are, for example, among the critical ethical issues being translated into regulatory standards and policies.

- Relationships among specialties in the counseling field are changing and require reevaluation of regulatory policies that affect the functional and structural relationships among areas of specialization. For example, substance abuse counseling and marriage and family counseling now need to be considered as specialties of counseling rather than as distinct professions with their own core areas of skill and knowledge.
- Regulations need revisions in view of research into the nature of complaints and outcomes of discipline cases. Complaints and violations in specific areas of improper conduct may not be effectively adjudicated due to poorly written statements of ethical and practice standards.
- Because our society constantly changes its expectations and definitions of the roles and functions of counselors and other behavioral science professionals, regulations must continually be evaluated to respond to these changes. Thus, for example, reporting requirements for child abuse have seen drastic changes, and managing potential injury and harm related to AIDS and sexual irresponsibility has become a counselor responsibility.
- Changes in the standards of, for example, professional training and supervised experience, examination requirements, and examination fees are all continually being evaluated during regulatory review. Costs to both applicants and the state are factors now playing a more important role in policy making.
- Responding to sunset legislation and providing administrative assurances that regulations are in compliance with legislative mandates, administrative process acts, or judicial decisions require an increasing amount of board time.

The Process of Change

The regulatory review process leading to revisions of regulations that govern the practice of counselors who are licensed, certified, or registered by a governmental agency such as a board of examiners is lengthy and typically takes at least 2 years to complete. It has two stages.

Stage 1: Public Participation in Regulatory Review. Regulatory changes generally must be instituted in compliance with an administrative process act defined by the state statutes. Such an act specifies the administrative rules and procedures for assuring that all board actions are legal and provide due process to those affected by the actions of a governmental agency such as a professional board.

One of the most important administrative process requirements associated with regulatory revision is holding public hearings on proposed regulatory changes with formal notice of intent to change professional regulations. Notification of public hearings on proposed regulatory reform takes many forms, and information on this process can be obtained from the appropriate state agency. The participation of individuals and professional associations is crucial to regulatory review and revision. Public hearings are excellent forums for professionals and consumers to share ideas and present research and suggestions for board consideration.

Regular attendance and representation at regulatory board meetings are recommended for every interested professional association. Association leaders and members need to know what is going on. An association member should serve as a liaison to the board and be responsible for keeping the association informed. Positive, nonadversarial relationships between the board and the professional associations must be built. Whenever regulation changes are being made, association input is valuable not only to professional counselors and their associations but also to the boards.

Stage 2: Promulgating Proposed Regulations. A valuable aspect of the regulatory review process is board reconciliation of proposed regulatory changes with public comment brought up at open hearings. The board is thus forced to reconcile its primary responsibility to protect the public with the ideals of the profession. The process of reconciliation may take the form of impact statements that can, for example, cover economic impact and professional access impact as well as analyze public policy.

Requirements for justifying proposed actions in view of public comment vary from board to board across the nation. Knowledge of the process is essential for any individual or professional group claiming interest and concern for the process of regulation of the counseling profession. If there is no significant public comment or input from concerned professionals, professional associations, or citizen groups, the board is left to make assessment of the needs of the consuming public and profession on its own. Private citizen, individual professional, and professional association involvement is critical to the success of regulatory review and change.

After public comments on proposed regulatory changes, justifications for proposed changes, and impact statements are analyzed, proposed regulations are generally published in a draft form. In some states, these drafts may be reviewed by a coordinating board. For example, in Virginia, final regulations must also undergo the scrutiny of a "super board"—the Board of Health Professions (BHP) of the Department of Health Professions. This board represents all health professions and the citizenry, exercises oversight, and coordinates the action of each health profession's board, although each health profession is represented on the BHP. Once the proposed regulations have been reviewed, comments may be made that must be considered before the proposed regulations are forwarded to the governor or other administrative office for final adoption and official promulgation.

Sunset Legislation and Legislative Changes to Existing Laws

Licensure, certification, and registration statutes are generally not permanent fixtures in state codes. Most governmental bodies have established mechanisms to evaluate the need to regulate a profession. This is as it should be. A regulatory mechanism to protect the public welfare should exist only to the extent that the exercise of a profession poses some potential for harm to the public. The need to regulate the counseling profession and the appropriate level of regulation should be periodically reviewed and evaluated.

Sunset legislation is a process requiring justification for continued regulation of a profession. State law simply states that each profession that is regulated shall be examined every so many years to see if it should continue to be regulated. This sunset review is always a critical issue in professional regulation because a board could be disbanded as a result of the review. Considerable emotional energy and economic concern are associated with this process of evaluating the continued need for the regulation, and/or level, of a particular credentialing board. The profession may see this process as a frontal attack on the very identity of the profession and of the professional. Professional boards come to respect the process as an inevitable aspect of accountability to the profession, the state, and the general public. Understanding the purpose, process, and the various avenues of involvement available enables individuals and associations to assist in meeting a sunset review. This can build positive relationships with the public, a professional board, and the governmental bodies responsible for appropriate recognition as licensed, certified, or registered professional counselors.

Criteria for Evaluating the Need for Professional Regulation

Most state professional regulatory agencies have invested considerable effort in developing a process for public policy analysis of health care provider regulation. Typically this process is based on criteria concerning risk or harm to the consumer, requirements for specialized skill and training, requirements for independent judgment and autonomous practice, uniqueness of scope of practice, economic impact, and least restrictive regulation.

Professional regulatory boards focus on such criteria to define or reevaluate the need to regulate or continue to regulate a profession when considering new statutory regulation or continuance of statutory regulation during a sunset review. Professional associations also focus on such criteria in defining or reevaluating needs for regulation or its continuance, in considering requests for new professional regulation, and in reviewing continued regulation of their profession. In the list that follows, criteria goals and action recommendations are included in order to suggest how professional counselors may use—and have used—each criterion in justifying the creation of credentialing boards and defending the continuation of licensure, certification, and registration laws.

1. **Risk or Harm to the Consumer**
    Goal: To demonstrate that the unregulated practice of the counseling profession will harm or endanger public health, safety, or welfare.
    Action Recommendations: Gather information concerning the 39 states in the nation that have regulatory laws governing the profession. Their histories of ethics complaints and disciplinary actions can provide a compelling statement of the potential and real harm associated with the practice of counseling. However, although case studies and testimonies tend to be more dramatic, they are most useful as supplemental data. Remember that regulatory administrators or legislators may be interested in national statistics, but data derived from your state's professional association or regulatory board are more impressive. In fact, risk to the consuming public cannot be argued well without data to support your position. Even though the risk may be evident to those in the counseling profession, others will be less than convinced in the absence of hard data on the potential and real harm to public health, safety, and welfare.

2. **Requirements for Specialized Skill and Training**
    Goal: To demonstrate that the practice of counseling requires specialized education, skills, and training and that the public needs to have the benefit of assured minimal professional competency.
    Action Recommendations: Establish a clear and convincing statement of the specialized body of knowledge, skills, and training that are required to assure minimal professional competency. Although the process of maintaining professional regulatory status or initiating regulation of a profession in a state where no regulation exists is a political process, and may involve turf battles, avoid as much as

possible any control of or influence on your thinking by the political process involved in gaining regulatory status or by the roles and functions of other helping professionals. The essential first step is developing a basic definition of the generic counseling process. This definitive statement should then be the foundation for delineating not only the unique aspects of the professional knowledge base but also the specialized skills, abilities, and training required to assure minimal professional competency.

It is also important to understand the historical foundation of the counseling profession, which is based on a developmental rather than a disease-oriented approach to mental health. A developmental tradition is not inconsistent with remedial and rehabilitative counseling functions, nor is it inconsistent with diagnostic formulations and treatment planning around DSM-IV (American Psychiatric Association, 1994) classifications.

Consider that use of the term *psychotherapy* in defining the role and function of professional counseling may be compelling for professional and economic reasons. *Psychotherapy,* however, is not an all-inclusive term defining the full scope of counseling practice but is a term that in part defines therapeutic functions shared by all behavioral science professions.

The following definition of the scope of practice of counseling defines who a licensed counselor is and what he or she does in Virginia. It also reflects outcomes of the effective working together of a state's regulatory board, legislature, and professional association to revise licensed professional counselor statutes in the Code of Virginia (1976, 1993).

> *Professional counselor* means a person trained in counseling interventions designed to facilitate an individual's achievement of human development goals and in remediating mental, emotional, or behavioral disorders and associated distresses which interfere with mental health and development. Counseling means the therapeutic process of (a) conducting assessments and diagnoses for the purpose of establishing treatment goals and objectives and (b) planning, implementing, and evaluating treatment plans using treatment interventions to facilitate human development and to identify and

remediate mental, emotional, or behavioral disorders and associated distresses which interfere with mental health. (Anderson, 1993)

3. **Requirements for Independent Judgment and Autonomous Practice**

   Goal: To establish the fact that the role of the counselor is one that requires independent professional judgment and that members of the profession function autonomously.

   Action Recommendations: An essential aspect of this criterion is the definition of the interpersonal technology of the helping process. Related to this is the professional discernment or independent clinical judgment of counselors required to execute their autonomous professional practice. Key areas of autonomous clinical judgment include assessment of developmental and remedial needs, assessment of personal resources and liabilities, clinical diagnosis, treatment planning, referral, consultation needs, and assessments of outcome.

4. **Uniqueness of Scope of Practice**

   Goal: To define the unique nature of the scope of practice of the counseling profession.

   Action Recommendations: Explore the question of how counseling is unique in role and function, especially in relationship to other professions. Difficulties arise because the behavioral sciences overlap in the central function of the therapeutic use of self in the interpersonal healing arts. Targets of treatment, theories or approaches, types of problems, or ways of conceptualizing client problems may help form a basis to define one behavioral science profession in relationship to another. There are social workers, clinical social workers, psychologists, school psychologists, and clinical psychologists. There are marriage and family counselors, mental health counselors, rehabilitation counselors, pastoral counselors, and substance abuse counselors. Where does the scope of one begin and the other end? Answers may be impossible, particularly in the often hostile arena of regulatory analysis. However, most professionals have taken the position that the professionals themselves, rather than regulatory bodies, should determine their own scope of practice based on their training, knowledge, and experience.

5. Economic Impact

Goal: To define the economic impact the proposed regulated profession will have on the profession and the public by asking, How will costs for services be affected by professional regulation that restricts access to a profession? What are the administrative costs of regulation? What will the licensee pay in fees, and are there other professional fees?

Action Recommendations: Be realistic and thorough. Investigate the costs of professional regulation and know the method for funding your state regulatory agency. Is it funded through government budget or will fees from regulated professionals offset expenses of regulation? Investigate the economic impact in your state of restricted providers of professional services. Counselors typically do not consider the dollars and cents of regulatory administration and the impact of regulation on the supply and demand of professional service providers.

6. Least Restrictive Regulation

Goal: To regulate a profession with the least restrictive influence on the profession that is consistent with protection of public health, safety, and welfare, and thus to consider realistically any alternative to regulation that might exist to achieve the goal of public protection.

Action Recommendations: There are several alternatives to occupational regulation that regulatory analysts and legislators will want to rule out before they regulate a profession. Some of these alternatives include consumer protection laws and regulations, inspection (discussed in the chapter on state regulatory credentials), disclosure requirements, and other mechanisms used to protect the public other than professional regulation. Provide a rational argument for the level of public protection deemed necessary. Remember that each legislator must understand how the level of real or potential harm is justified by the level of regulation proposed. Make sure the definitions of scope of practice and the risk to the public are well documented so that regulations can be based on the data provided.

How a Credentialing Bill Becomes Law

Once research on the criteria discussed in the preceding section
has been completed, a bill can be drafted. Bills may be introduced by a counseling association or group, or as a part of an
administrative legislative initiative by a credentialing board or
oversight agency of government. (This latter method often takes
the form of a governor's bill.) An ideal situation is for a credentialing
bill to be introduced by a credentialing board or oversight
agency in cooperation with and supported by the professional
association. The bill needs a house, senate, or administration
sponsor. The broader the sponsorship of a bill the greater the
chances it will be passed. Bills introduced into the legislature
are routinely assigned to a legislative committee in which the
merits of the bill are discussed. The legislative committee may
pass, kill, amend, or ignore the bill. Influencing legislative
committee action on a desired credentialing bill is critical. The
consulting fees of good lobbyists and attorneys can be well worth
the investment needed to get a bill out of legislative committee
for a reading before the full house or senate.

When a bill is presented before the full house and senate for
a hearing and vote, every member of the profession across the
state or nation becomes critical to the bill's passage or defeat.
Because of the unpredictable nature of the legislative hearing
and voting process, an instant communication network—using
telephone and facsimile (fax) machines—is essential. Planning
for massive political involvement on the days and at the critical
hours of committee and full house and senate hearings debate
and voting must be done months and even a year ahead. A clear
voice of the profession in support of a credentialing bill or
against the bill must be heard (almost instantaneously) and
whenever needed. The degree of coordination and planning that
is needed requires a well-financed political action committee
and the support of lobbyists and experienced political action
coordinators who are committed to an association's political
action goals.

Remember that both houses of the legislature must pass
similar bills. Often there is considerable compromise and modi-
fication. Lobbying by the profession is critical. Once the bill has
passed both chambers, the bill is then sent to the executive office

for the governor's signature. Here again, lobbying and political action to ensure the signing of a bill are critical. Finally, if the governor vetoes the bill, the legislature can overturn the veto in most states. Only with active participation in the legislative process, and justifying the need for credentialing legislation, can a counselor credentialing bill become law!

 # Reciprocity and Endorsement

Americans usually live in several states over the course of their work lives. The American professional worker is probably the most mobile of all the nation's occupational groups. Thus credentialing and occupational mobility in the counseling profession are among the most pressing national and international issues facing the growing profession. As Young (1987) observed, "Licensing laws can create maldistributions in the supply of practitioners, especially when laws make it difficult for licensed professionals in one state to obtain a license in another" (p. 59).

Young also commented that factors other than credentialing differences across the nation could contribute to unequal distributions of occupational groups. Some of those factors include differences in earning potential, educational opportunities, per capita income, and population distribution. Even geography, culture, and climate may have an influence.

Another aspect of this issue is the effect of differing standards of credentialing, which may make it more difficult to move to another state and continue a professional practice. Reciprocity and endorsement are two regulatory processes that can contribute to professional mobility and the transfer of occupational rights to practice counseling among the states.

Reciprocity, which is the stronger and more valuable component of the regulatory process, requires a formal agreement among credentialing bodies that individuals who are credentialed in one state will be credentialed in another state as requested. For complete reciprocity across the nation, all regulatory boards must adopt the concept of comparable roles, functions, education, training, experience, examination processes, and standards, and agree to accept one set of credentialing requirements. Achieving national credentialing reciprocity in the counseling profession is a monumental challenge now confronting the profession and ACA. However, in spite of political obstacles, attaining the uniform requirements that facilitate reciprocity is well worth the effort for both practitioners and consumers.

Most state boards, by statute or as part of regulatory policy, currently provide at least some form of reciprocity. This is generally stated in terms of meeting equivalent requirements. However, the applicants must themselves determine whether the requirements they have met are the equivalent (or higher) because in no case are specific states named. An examination of basic knowledge is common to all, but requirements for graduate credit hours, supervision hours, and actual practice are diverse.

Within the counseling profession itself, a process of standardizing professional requirements appears to be operating, which should enable the reciprocity process. For example, ACA recommends a minimum of 60 graduate semester hours and 2 years or 3,000 hours of supervision (Bloom et al., 1990). The requirements for the clinical specialty certification as CCMHC are at approximately the same level. In addition, many states have reached or are approaching (and even surpassing) the recommended minimum. Pressure was long exerted by NACCHMC—and is now by the NBCC, with which the academy merged in July 1993—for all credentialed counselors to reach the minimum level not only for the sake of uniformity but also to ensure better trained therapists for the public and to meet minimal requirements of reimbursers as well as to attain a uniform professional level across the nation.

In related professions, such as social work and psychology, the trend is also to increase entry-level requirements for licensure. Attempts to credential at lower levels, possibly with a different title (such as psychologist's aide), have generally been unsuccessful.

The rapidly increasing use nationwide of the NBCC's National Counselor Examination as the basic knowledge examination is further promoting reciprocity. More than half the states that now license counselors use this examination; and applicants who pass the examination both fulfill a requirement for state licensure and for NBCC certification as a National Certified Counselor.

The American Association of State Counseling Boards (AASCB), which was established to assist board members in regulating the counseling profession, has as a goal addressing the need for better national coordination of efforts to achieve reciprocity among the states in the counseling profession. The difficulties of achieving the goal are exemplified by boards, such as those in Georgia, Ohio, and Washington, that issue licenses to more than one profession and at different levels. Nevertheless, the efforts of AASCB and its members, who are representatives from state counseling credentialing bodies, in coordination with ACA, CACREP, and other national professional organizations, should prove fruitful in the 1990s.

Endorsement, the second regulatory process that can contribute to professional mobility and transfer of occupational rights for counselors, is a unilateral administrative policy of a regulatory board to recognize the qualifications of a credentialed counselor and grant a license or certificate to practice. If a credentialing board of a state finds that applicants from another state meet or exceed their standards for education, training, and experience, that state may unilaterally grant an endorsement of a credential based on this fact. This type of unilateral administrative process of recognizing comparable standards can increase the mobility of professionals, thereby providing services in states needing professional counselors. Unilateral endorsement policies could be used as needed as a good substitute for the more desirable national (and possibly international) reciprocity agreements.

 # Complaints Against Counselors

Few professional challenges compare with the emotional intensity and level of concern created by having to defend personal and professional integrity against charges of unprofessional conduct in a forum of professional peers or in a court of law. This is why counsel should be contacted immediately upon learning of a complaint being filed or a suit being brought so that an adequate defense may be prepared. An attorney is especially valuable in the mental health area because of the emotional and personal relation and private nature of the counseling process.

In the case of a complaint and resulting charge of misconduct, all aspects of an otherwise private and interpersonally intense process become exposed to microscopic scrutiny by the professional board, peer professionals, the courts (if a civil action is brought), and often even the public. Even when there are findings of "no violation," and certainly when there are findings of impropriety and misconduct, results are at the least distressing and potentially devastating to the involved (accused) counselor.

An important benefit of credentialing is the establishment of standards of professional preparation and conduct. One potentially devastating end result of credentialing, however, is being held accountable for professional misconduct or, for consumers of counseling services, becoming aware of being the victim of professional incompetence or misconduct. Certainly, it is best that such incidents of professional evaluation and possible disciplinary action never occur, both for the client and the counselor. However, evidence is clear that complaints are increasing: Both the cost of malpractice insurance and the number of convictions of incompetent, impaired, and/or irresponsible counselors are on the rise. Credentialing means standards, and standards result in analysis of events, evaluation, and judgment. A benefit of credentialing in counseling is professional identity, pride, and consumer praise. The other side of the coin is the criticism of not meeting professional standards or consumer expectations.

ACA's Task Force on Impaired Counselors (Anderson, Swanson, & Talbutt, 1992) completed a study of disciplinary problems brought before state boards 1990-92. This study showed that the majority of violations (32%) involved unlicensed activity or practice, that is, counselors who had not attained licensure or certification. Unprofessional conduct involving dual relationships, substance abuse, intimate involvement with clients, use of offensive language, and other offenses comprised 26% of violations. Violations of professional standards of practice ranked third in percentage. Sexual abuse of clients was found in 8% of cases reported.

One board reported that its discipline committee imposed sanctions against professional counselors that ranged from suspensions (15%) and revocation of licenses (13%) to no sanctions (3%) and reprimand and warning (23%).

Further data reported by the ACA Task Force on Impaired Counselors indicate that more experienced boards with a history of involvement in professional discipline had a higher rate of disciplinary action than newer boards. The incidence of charges seems uniform and involves about 3% of licensees.

Who Receives and Processes Complaints?

ACA's *Ethical Standards* (AACD, 1988) provide the foundation for ethical standards of the national voluntary credentialing agencies. Other credentialing bodies such as the American

Association for Marriage and Family Therapy (1991) and the National Board for Certified Counselors (1989) also provide ethical standards for professional conduct. It is under these basic ethical standards that a complaint (against a credentialed counselor) is evaluated at the national level.

Although the ethical standards of professional associations may serve the need to evaluate conduct of its voluntarily credentialed membership, state boards of counseling are in a slightly different position. Ethical standards, as expressed by professional groups, represent the ideal. A professional code of ethics is a standard of conduct that a practitioner voluntarily chooses to adhere to as a result of a personal desire to affiliate with a group. The act of voluntary membership through seeking a credential is a choice to accept the standards of the body and to be subject to disciplinary actions of that body.

The state credential is generally considered involuntary as compared with a voluntary credential on a national level, such as the NCC. The state board, unlike voluntary credentialing bodies, must define legally defensible criteria for revoking, suspending, or otherwise curtailing the professional property right of an individual to engage in the practice of his or her profession. Standards of practice or ethical codes of conduct that form the basis for disciplinary actions by a state board must meet two important legal criteria that codes of voluntary credentialing groups may not meet: (1) the standard of practice must be directly related to a potential harm to the public, and (2) the standard of practice must be legally defensible based on a performance standard that can be clearly evaluated rather than ideally stated.

Standards of practice expressed in codes of ethics establish consumer expectations as well as expectations among members of the counseling profession. When those expectations of performance are violated or unmet, a basis for a complaint exists. The ACA (1981) standard for professional conduct, Section A-3, states that:

> Ethical behavior among professional associates, both members and nonmembers, must be expected at all times. When information is possessed that raises doubt as to the ethical behavior of professional colleagues, whether Association members or not, the member must take action to rectify such a condition. Such

action shall use the institution's channels first and then use procedures established by the Association. (AACD, 1988, Sec. A)

This statement clearly places the responsibility for policing the profession on the shoulders of each member. Similar statements are found in other professional association codes. What exactly does this mean for those associated with various credentialing processes across the nation? What are the institutional channels described in the ACA code? How are ethical violations resolved? What are the responsibilities of counselors in regard to ethical practice?

First and most obvious, counselors must know the ethical codes of their professional groups. Counselors must thus

- be able to evaluate and manage their own professional behavior;
- be able to evaluate the behaviors of other professionals;
- assume responsibility for the enforcement of standards of practice in the profession;
- assume responsibility for constructive action in response to information of professional impairment or misconduct;
- recognize the relationship between institutional demands and ethical standards of practice; evaluate institutional resources, policies, and procedures that may be appropriate in addressing ethical violations and in resolving them;
- recognize and act in accordance with the profession's compelling interest for the health, safety, and welfare of consumers, regardless of the setting within which these services are offered;
- appreciate the fact that a problem that is resolved is no longer a problem; take all available actions necessary to immediately rectify ethical violations;
- report any violation of professional ethics to the disciplinary committee of the professional body whose standards have been violated;
- assist the credentialing body to understand the extent of their actions to rectify the ethical violation and the nature of the condition that has given rise to the complaint of ethical violation.

Ethical violations presented to an association or state board are usually investigated through varying levels of informal fact finding, hearings, and investigations. State boards typically have telephone hotlines for complaints. A valid complaint is usually followed by an informal investigation or fact-finding hearing in which facts surrounding the complaint are gathered. Findings of fact may be established at the informal hearing level, and action appropriate to the violation taken. Such action may be the dismissal of a complaint with no violation found, or a sanction against a counselor because of a finding of a violation of professional standards. Many complaints are resolved at these less-formal fact-finding levels.

Formal administrative hearings are usually associated with more complex cases in which findings of fact are challenged by a party to the complaint. Typically, attorneys, court reporters, a full discipline committee, administrative hearing officer, and/ or full credentialing board with witnesses and professional experts may be involved in a formal hearing of professional misconduct.

Formal disciplinary hearings often involve controversial points of administrative law, strong emotions, and constant reference to standards of professional practice. The process is a severe personal and professional challenge even when the outcome is no violation. A finding of a violation can mean the literal end of a career, an indefinite revocation of a license or certificate, and expulsion from the profession. Other actions of a credentialing body include such sanctions as a reprimand, a stayed revocation, a fine, mandated continuing education, supervision or treatment for professional impairment, and/or temporary suspension of the license or other credential.

Actions of a state board are not, as standard administrative policy, reported to voluntary credentialing bodies or vice versa. Disciplinary committees of boards and ethics committees of credentialing bodies and professional associations function independently. Some formal reciprocal interagency notification process seems needed and desirable to assure that those found incompetent, irresponsible, or impaired are restrained from continued practice. The goal of achieving such an intercredentialing body reporting system may well be achieved through cooperation of ACA and AAACB in the near future.

Responding to Complaints Filed Against You

If you find that a complaint has been filed against you, it should not be a surprise. Most complaints come from dissatisfied clients or as a result of confrontations about your behavior with other professionals. All charges should be taken very seriously by the counselor, and legal advice and assistance sought immediately. Any valid complaint or statement of concern or dissatisfaction is, therefore, an opportunity to improve as a professional. Complaints that have no validity constitute a terrible hassle, yet may be a valuable learning experience. Both serve to sensitize you to the reality that a counselor's action is judged by standards that must be upheld. Responding to complaints with a positive attitude toward concerns expressed by a colleague or a client is critical to achieving a favorable outcome. Not all complaints result in the finding of a violation.

Always seek to resolve problems at the lowest level possible without compromise of personal and professional integrity. Never attempt to continue treating a client who uses the threat of legal action to manipulate. Certainly, never attempt to treat a client who is pursuing legal actions against you. Document all activity related to your actions in order to defend yourself against a potential complaint.

Once a complaint has been filed, cooperate fully in investigations and seek competent legal counsel on matters of legal concern. Do not underestimate the seriousness of a complaint of unprofessional conduct and take a cavalier attitude to the process. Defend your actions if you feel that what you have done is defensible. Analyze your behavior in relationship to the standards of practice by which you are being evaluated. Consult with other professionals about your behavior and your level of personal functioning. Respect the conclusions and advice that are offered and act positively on this counsel.

Finally, you may either accept findings of fact and conclusions of the board or appeal to a higher tribunal. Don't accept a decision at this "trial" level unless you are totally satisfied. Consultation with your attorney about the ramifications of any decision is a must. Remember that if a complaint is filed against you, it is possible that the professional liability insurance policy you hold may provide legal consultation and representation for you. Check the terms of your policy.

Third-Party Reimbursement and Cost Consciousness

Professional counselors may be reimbursed for their services directly by their clients or by a third-party payer. These third parties, discussed in depth in Volume 9 of the ACA Legal Series (Strosnider & Grad, 1993), may be the major health reimbursement plans such as Blue Cross/Blue Shield, Civilian Health and Medical Program of the Uniformed Services (CHAMPUS), Medicare, Medicaid, and Federal Employees Health Benefits Program. Third parties may also be private insurers and self-insured companies. With increasing frequency, third parties include or involve managed care organizations.

As of 1993, nine states mandate insurance reimbursement for professional counselors (Strosnider & Grad, 1993). Of the remaining states, some make no provision for reimbursement of professional counselors, but others have freedom-of-choice legislation that mandates reimbursement of various health care practitioners, including counselors. This type of legislation has been passed to give the consuming public the choice of more than one type of professional for the treatment of, for example, mental or emotional disorders. Thus insurance companies that are licensed to do business within such a state must reimburse clients for the services of certain licensed professionals, which may include counselors.

Licensure is normally one of the requirements for all third-party reimbursement. Others may be specific *DSM-IV* diagnoses, mental health coverage of the insurance purchaser, certain reports (which may include prognosis and progress reports), and a provider number obtained from the insurer.

Few counselors could maintain a private practice without third-party payments. Few insurers voluntarily pay nonmandated benefits, and prospective clients tend to seek care for which they will be reimbursed.

The trend to managed health care is increasingly important for counselors to explore and understand. Managed health care organizations are affecting not only reimbursement but also what types of care are provided. *Managed care* is an umbrella term for various methods used by corporations and, in turn, insurers, to reduce the spiraling costs of health care, including mental health care. Health care costs have risen from $39 billion and 6% of the gross national product (GNP) in 1965 to over $500 billion and 12.5% of the GNP at present (Broskowski, 1991). Drug abuse and mental health costs have risen at an even higher rate than medical costs, jumping from between 2 and 5% to nearly 20%.

In an effort to cut these costs, programs with such titles as case management organization (CMO), health maintenance organization (HMO), preferred provider organization (PPO), and employee assistance program (EAP) have been established. PPOs are a particularly rapidly growing force in the mental health field. To provide counseling at the lowest possible cost, these organizations seek licensed professionals with a firm commitment to solution-focused, six- to eight-session, short-term therapy and outpatient treatment. Treatment plans may be continuously reviewed to assure adherence to this philosophy.

The impact of these managed care organizations is already being felt. Professional counselors need to explore this cost-cutting movement that strives for least intrusive care (that is, outpatient as opposed to hospitalization). Training programs, state boards, and national credentialing organizations need to examine the effects of this potent influence for change on the counseling process and service providers. Are professional counselors meeting the challenge of managed mental health care?

What special training may be needed? Are new approaches to therapy going to be necessary? Are present examinations able to determine an applicant's capability to utilize short-term therapy successfully? All training programs and all credentialing bodies may need to re-think both the theoretical aspects of standard practice and the measures of competency that they require of licensees.

Because counseling professionals have long recognized the effectiveness of short-term therapy, as contrasted with extensive, expensive, analytical systems, they can be in the forefront of these efforts. One of the greatest challenges to the counseling profession in the 1990s may well be the cost consciousness that is the absolute demand of third-party reimbursers in their efforts to save dollars in the mental health field.

Another, related challenge may be the counseling profession's need to determine minimum professional competency. The demands for efficiency inherent in managed health care, as well as consumer demands for specialized competency and full disclosure, may provide the impetus for more rigorous training and better screening of would-be practitioners.

Frequently Asked Questions

Q. Why should I get licensed if I don't have to?

A. At some point in time your state may require all counselors to be licensed even though it does not at present. You're preparing for the future! The license lets the consuming public know you have certain qualifications and shows your support of both the credentialing process and your profession. You are also telling the state (legislators, administrative departments, and board officers) that licensure of your profession is important.

In addition, a license gives you more career flexibility. Usually there are many more doors open to the licensee than to the uncredentialed person. Being licensed enhances client-counselor relationships as well as professional status. A license is also needed, in most cases, if you are interested in seeking third-party payments. Another important benefit of being licensed is legal protection for privileged communication.

Q. What is the difference between state licensure and national certification?

A. The state license is issued by a governmental unit of your state and allows you to practice your profession in your state. (It may be a criminal act to practice without a license.) Reimbursement for your professional services is normally dependent on your holding a license. National certification is provided by your professional associations, either directly or indirectly, and shows, like licensure, that you have met basic criteria established for the practice of your profession. It is not required by state laws. However, this credential lets the public know that you have been professionally recognized by a national, professional credentialing agency. It is also a sign that you support your profession and feel that the standards it has set are worthwhile.

Q. What is the difference between my certification as a school counselor and state licensure?

A. The issuing bodies are two different branches of government, one being your state department of education and the other, generally, being a department of health or health professions. Your school certificate allows you to practice within the school system, and the license allows you to practice in the private sector. There is no crossover here; that is, your license does not allow you to become a school counselor and your school certificate does not permit you to practice in the private sector for a fee. Keep in mind that preparation and credentialing standards are different due to different emphases, even though there may be a common core of requirements for both credentials.

Q. Why do I have to get another license if I move to a different state?

A. Unfortunately, states have different requirements and therefore may not accept the license you already hold. (This is true of virtually all professions.) Often, however, an examination may be waived if the two states are using the same national exam (such as the National Counselor Examination given by the National Board for Certified Counselors). Even if complete reciprocity should come about, an individual state may still require you to apply and become licensed if you are going to practice in that state. Reciprocity will certainly expedite the process and eliminate the duplication of a great deal of the paper work. States will always, though, run certain checks on applicants to make sure they have not lost a license in another state and that they are legally qualified for a license.

Q. What is the difference between my university being accredited and my graduate program being accredited?

A. Basically, your university needs accreditation to exist. This accreditation looks at the whole university—all disciplines, all levels—from a broad point of view. Accreditation of your graduate program means that it has met standards developed specifically for the discipline of counseling. Here specific standards pertaining to the quality of faculty, facilities, and actual course work offered must be met. This process goes into greater depth than university-wide accreditation. Departmental or program accreditation looks, in detail, at the professional needs of a specific graduate training program.

Q. Can I say I graduated from an accredited program if it was accredited after I graduated?

A. Technically, no. The program was not accredited at the time you studied there. It may, however, be helpful to be able to say that the program you attended is now accredited.

Q. Where can I find the requirements for licensure in my state?

A. An update is given each year in the archival section of the *Journal of Counseling and Development* published by the American Counseling Association. Current addresses and phone numbers of the boards or contact persons are given. Further information may be obtained by contacting the Advocacy Office at ACA headquarters. In most states the office of the secretary of state can give you this information. You also should be able to obtain more in-depth information from your state counseling association.

Q. Why do state licensure boards use a national, written exam?
A. This is a big step towards reciprocity, a step many professions have taken. It gives credence to the entire profession by having

one exam that is relevant and valid in every state that credentials counselors. It is also cheaper for all concerned. The cost of developing, validating, and updating a professional examination is tremendous. Smaller states found they could not afford the cost. It is also less costly to the applicant in that it can suffice for both national voluntary certification and state licensure. Finally, it is a mark of a mature profession and a unifying factor within the profession. It also tends to make the cost more equal to all applicants.

 # Guidelines
for Practice

When you are considering credentials . . .

1. Study carefully the benefits and disadvantages of all available credentials.
2. Ask yourself, for example, Do I need this one? What will it cost? Will it benefit the public or my profession? Could I benefit personally from the attainment of this certificate?

If you are a student in counselor training . . .

1. Learn the requirements for all credentials early in your program.
2. Find out what you need in the way of course work, practicums, internships, and supervised experience.
3. Determine which credential(s) will help you attain your career goals.
4. Take required examination(s) soon after graduation while the course work is still fresh in your mind if possible
5. See in what ways you can have input into the requirements for credentialing, and go to work!

In keeping up with changes in the field . . .

1. Urge your board or national credentialing agency to keep you and your colleagues posted on changes in regulations and laws

that may have a bearing on your practice. Ask to be on their public notice mailing list to receive information regarding hearings and meetings concerning regulation changes. Too many practitioners are not aware of statutes in their own state that have an impact on their profession. Stay informed and involved.

2. Ask your state's professional counseling association to provide information regularly on credentialing through newsletters, conferences, and programs.

In determining renewal requirements . . .

1. See if requirements for renewal of your credential require continuing education. If so, keep an accurate record of your training, including convention workshops, seminars, and graduate courses in the manner prescribed by your board.
2. Be sure you keep your address current with your board.

To keep up with the effects of politics on credentialing . . .

1. Be aware of the political process, the ins and outs, which have a great impact on state credentialing.
2. Find out what you can do within this process to effect change, if needed, and to secure professional regulation if your state does not yet license counselors.
3. Learn how your legislature works and where the power is within that body.

To become an active, involved professional . . .

1. Join your state counselors association and ACA, if you haven't yet.
2. Stay active within your association(s).
3. Keep up with the professional literature, including the newspapers, such as *Guidepost* or *The Advocate,* and the ACA journals. Such publications give excellent coverage of all issues affecting your professional credentials. Examples of informative articles include Covin, 1991a, 1991b, 1992a, 1992b, 1993; Glosoff, 1992a, 1992b; Remley, 1991, 1992, 1993a, 1993b; and Vroman and Bloom, 1991.
4. Seek out opportunities to be heard, and to listen, at state and national counseling conventions.

Summary

In the credentialing field it is difficult, if not impossible, to separate legal, ethical, and professional issues. They go hand in hand in the establishment of regulations and requirements for licensure, certification, or registration. Credentials issued by either state governments or national professional agencies incorporate legal statutes, administrative regulations, and ideals of professional practice to define, govern, and control the counseling profession.

Credentials issued by states may be legally required in order to practice counseling. They may take the form of licensure, certification, or registration. Licensure is the highest form of regulation and usually gives title protection as well as the right to practice. It is enacted in order to provide maximum public protection where potential for public harm is greatest. Benefits that accrue to practitioners through licensure often include privileged communication as well as freedom-of-choice legislation, which provides for reimbursement to the professional counselor by third-party insurers.

National credentialing is voluntary and generally is called *certification*. An example of national certification is the National Certified Counselor (NCC) certificate from the National Board for Certified Counselors (NBCC). Professional associations such as ACA have been instrumental in establishing these certifying agencies, which have become free-standing or at least semiautonomous agencies that independently control the issuance of certificates. Although voluntary, national professional associations strongly urge their members to become certified to enhance their professionalism and the profession.

One important outcome of the credentialing movement has been drawing counselors into the political arena. A greater awareness of the political process has been achieved as the very existence of counseling as a profession in some states has depended on securing counselor credentialing legislation. Professional associations, such as ACA, are not only active in the counselor licensing movement but also in securing legislation providing for privileged communication and third-party payments to counselors. Counselors must maintain a politically active role in the process of government at the federal and state levels. This is especially true today because of the massive changes underway in mental health care financing and coverage. Counselors must be covered by national legislation providing for mental health care; credentialing of counselors across the nation is essential to achieving this goal.

The credentialing goal for today includes the licensure of counselors in all states and uniform recognition of certified, licensed counselors by the federal government as fully qualified mental health care providers with special expertise to offer the public. A further goal is the attainment of credentialing reciprocity among all states. Such uniformity will help secure public recognition of professional counselors as integral providers in the mental health service delivery system.

 # Discussion Questions

1. Is licensing beneficial to counselors? Does the quality of services improve after licensing laws are passed?

2. Does a license specify the types of clients or problems the practitioner is competent to deal with? Are the techniques a counselor may use limited by the license?

3. After working 12 years as a school counselor, what do I need in order to be licensed? Will graduate credits earned 12 years ago and school experience count toward the license?

4. Are the counselors who have obtained a license required to demonstrate competent performance as a condition for licensure renewal?

5. Is continuing education, training, or supervision required of licensees?

6. Are there any advantages or disadvantages for a school counselor to be licensed? For a college counselor?

7. Are there levels of licensure in the counseling profession? If so, what special qualifications are required?

8. What are the requirements for a license as a counselor? Should I concentrate in one area, such as marriage and family therapy or substance abuse counseling, in my studies? Do I need to take all my course work in one institution?

9. What is the employment outlook for licensed professional counselors over the next 10 years?

10. Who regulates the licensure or certification of a counselor?

11. What are the most important professional competencies required for licensure as a counselor?

12. If I am licensed, am I more likely to be held liable for any actions of mine that might have caused harm to my client(s)?

13. Are there any laws that protect licensed counselors from prosecution in the courts?

14. Can schools or other agencies be held legally liable if they permit personnel who are inadequately trained to perform counseling or psychotherapy?

15. When making referrals, how can I be sure the person I am referring to is competent and ethical? Do I need to know if the person is licensed?

16. Can an educational institution be held liable for any training its students receive that later may cause harm to their clients?

Suggested Readings

Anderson, D. (February, 1993). Professional counseling: Poised for the year 2000. *Virginia Counselors Journal, 21,* 69-76. An account of the efforts of the Virginia Board of Professional Counselors and Virginia Association of Clinical Counselors to amend a 17-year-old statutory definition of professional counseling.

Bloom, J., et al. (1990). Model legislation for licensed professional counselors. *Journal of Counseling and Development, 68,* 511-523. A suggested statement for use in drafting counselor licensure legislation. The article describes the ideal bill including rationale.

Brooks, D. K., Jr., & Gerstein, L. H. (1990). Counselor credentialing and interprofessional collaboration. *Journal of Counseling and Development, 68,* 477-484. A case for collaboration by counselors with other mental health professions in the credentialing field. The authors argue that broader issues affecting all the helping professionals take precedence over narrow turf issues.

Forrest, D. V., & Affemann, M. (1986). The future for mental health counselors in health maintenance organizations. *AMHCA Journal, 8,* 65-72.

Gibson, W. T., & Pope, K. S. (1993, January/February). The ethics of counseling: A national survey of certified counselors. *Journal of Counseling and Development, 71*(3), 330-336. A research report on the National Board for Certified Counselors indicating perceptions of ethical behaviors, levels of confidence in perceptions, and sources of information on professional ethics.

Hopkins, B. R., & Anderson, B. J. (1990). *The counselor and the law* (3rd ed.). Alexandria, VA: American Association for Counseling and Development. General information about how the law affects the counselor and helpful do's and don'ts.

Hummel, D. L., Talbut, L. C., & Alexander, M. D. (1985). *Law and ethics in counseling*. New York: Van Nostrand Reinhold. A complete, concisely written summary of the ethical principles and laws governing the practice of counseling.

Spruill, D. A., & Fong, M. L. (1990). Defining the domain of mental health counseling: From identity confusion to consensus. *Journal of Mental Health Counseling, 12*(1), 12-23. A review of the literature describing the role, models, and essential knowledge and skills of the mental health counselor. The profession is then defined based on the literature review.

Weikel, W. J., & Palmo, A. J. (1980). The evolution and practice of mental health counseling. *Journal of Mental Health Counseling, 11*(1), 7-25. An examination of the growth of the profession and its future, including descriptions of roles, identity and ethical issues, and private practice and training issues.

References

Alberding, B., Lauver, P., & Patnoe, J. (1993). Counselor awareness of the consequences of certification and licensure. *Journal of Counseling and Development, 72*(1), 33–38.

American Association for Counseling and Development. (1988). *Ethical standards.* Alexandria, VA: Author

American Association for Marriage and Family Therapy. (1991). *AAMFT code of ethics.* Washington, DC: Author.

American Psychiatric Association. (1994). *Diagnostic and statistical manual of mental disorders* (4th ed.). (DSM-IV). Washington, DC: Author

Anderson, D. (1993, February). Professional counseling: Poised for the year 2000. *Virginia Counselors Journal, 21,* 69–76.

Anderson, D., Swanson, C. D., Talbutt, L. C. (1992, June). Report of the Task Force on the Impaired Counselor to the ACA Governing Council. Alexandria, VA: American Counseling Association.

Annotated Code of Maryland, Health Occupations, Sec. 17, 101–502.1 (1985).

Arizona Code, Sec. 32, 3251–3301 (1988, 1989).

Bloom, J., et al. (1990). Model legislation for licensed professional counselors. *Journal of Counseling and Development, 68,* 511–523.

Broskowski, A. (1991). Current mental health care environments: Why managed care is necessary. *Professional Psychology: Research and Practice, 22*(1), 6–14.

Clawson, T. W. (1991). Certification and licensure. *NBCC News Notes, 8*(3).

Code of Virginia, Sec. 54.0 (1976).

Code of Virginia, Sec. 5.2 (1987).

Code of Virginia, Sec. 54.1 (1993).

Covin, T. M. (1991a). Freedom of choice and CHAMPUS: An update. *The Advocate, 14,* 10.

Covin, T. M. (1992a). Freedom of choice and definitions of mental health counseling. *The Advocate, 15*(6), 3.

Covin, T. M. (1991b). Freedom of choice and medicine. *The Advocate, 15,* 1.

Covin, T. M. (1992b). Freedom of choice and statutory regulation. *The Advocate, 16*(1), 3

Covin, T. M. (1992b). Freedom of choice and uniform national standards for MHCs. *The Advocate, 16*(5), 3.

Garcia, A. (1990). An examination of the social work professions' efforts to achieve legal regulation. *Journal of Counseling and Development, 68*(5), 491-497.

Glosoff, H.L. (1992a). Accrediting and certifying professional counselors. *Guidepost, 34*(12), 6–8.

Glosoff, H.L. (1992b). Professional advocacy: Counselors advocating for themselves. *Guidepost, 34*(11), 6.

National Association of Alcoholism and Drug Abuse Counselors. (1990, July–August). A national credential for counselors. *The Counselor,* p. 7.

National Board for Certified Counselors. (1993). CCMHC becomes NBCC's fourth specialty. *News Notes, 10*(1).

National Board for Certified Counselors. (1989). *Code of ethics.* Alexandria, VA: American Association for Counseling and Development.

Remley, T. P., Jr. (1991). Perspectives: Why licensure? *Guidepost, 34*(5).

Remley, T. P., Jr. (1992). Perspectives. *Guidepost, 34*(7).

Remley, T. P., Jr. (1993a). Perspectives: Uniformity in licensure. *Guidepost, 36*(1).

Remley, T. P., Jr. (1993b). Perspectives. *Guidepost, 36*(2).

Romano, G. (1992). The power and pain of professionalization. *American Counselor, 1*(1), 16–23.

Strosnider, J.S., & Grad, J.D. (1993). *Third-party payments* (ACA Legal Series, Vol. 9). Alexandria, VA: American Counseling Association.

Vroman, C.S., & Bloom, J.W. (1991). A summary of counselor credentialing legislation. In F.O. Bradley (Ed.), *Credentialing in counseling* (pp. 86–102). Alexandria, VA: American Association for Counseling and Development.

Young, D. S. (1987). *The rule of experts: Occupational licensing in America.* Washington, DC: Cato Institute.